Love Notes

by
Velvet Musings

ISBN: 9798281810302

DEDICATION:

to love and loving

CONTENTS

Introduction:

In the quiet spaces between heartbeats, where
souls whisper and love linger, there exists a love
so sacred, a bond so secure no distance can sever -
a melody, a divine harmony that binds two spirits
as one.

Some loves are written in the stars – etched into
the cosmos before time began, destined to burn
brighter than a thousand suns. In these pages love
is not just an emotion – it is a sacred thread,
woven through trials and triumph, stitched
together with movements of joy, solitude, solace,
and devotion. This is the love that lingers and
interspersed in the written lines of Love Notes – a
collection of tender verses, a symphony of
whispered affections, sacred promises, and the
devotion that defies the boundaries of existence.
These poems are more than just words – they are
the heartbeat of a love so deep, so boundless, that
the universe pauses to listen. The words are
designed to celebrate a love that does not falter –
a love that is felt in the deepest parts of the soul,
where no distance or time can divide. Here in
these pages, you will find the devotion – of being

wholly cherished, endlessly adored, deeply desired, and spiritually connected in a way that transcends time.

Here is a space created for the lovers who have known the ache of separation, who have weathered storms of stillness, and the solace often found only in prayers and silence. You will find that the deepest parts of you are cherished, easily adored, and worthy of devotion. Love Notes hope to cradle you, consume you, remind you that you are adored beyond measure – that your love is a force that bends the universe.

Your journey into Love Notes will be where you understand that love is a covenant –written in love, sealed with quiet power, a simple gaze that sees straight into the depths of who you are. These written words are a psalm for the beloved, hymns of a profound connection that trembles in the perfection of love, a desire so deep the earth it becomes a storm, This is the love that angels proclaim for you –the love that doesn't fade, but transforms, deepening as you grow through and in love.

Let these words be the mirror that reflects your soul's truth: you are cherished by design, adored

without condition, and bound to your beloved by something greater than chance. Love is not just felt in grand gestures, but in the quiet certainty that no matter where love leads, you are never alone.
You are held. You are beloved. You are wanted.
You are love.

ACKNOWLEDGMENTS:

Past, Present and Future Loves

Thank you for the love we received, the love we thought we needed and the love we desired.

Velvet Musings

Love Notes
by
Velvet Musings

Romantic

There is a particular magic in the beginning of love. A spark that flares and warms everything that it touches. These poems live in that glow, when two hearts discover each other. This section is an ode to the sweetness of romantic love. The euphoria of newness, the pull of a glance held too long and the rush of possibilities.

Here love unfolds gently. There is a softness in the way we come to know another soul. How affection deepens in intimacy, how small gestures begin to mean everything. It's in the trust built word by word, the slow dance of vulnerability, and the choice to stay.

These poems do not shy away from the dream of love. They embrace its fantasy. The space where flaws are softened by affection. Where hope whispers Here love unfolds gently. There is a softness in the way we come to know another soul. How affection deepens in intimacy, how small gestures begin to mean everything. It's in the trust built word by word, the slow dance of vulnerability, and the choice to stay.

These poems do not shy away from the dream of love. They embrace its fantasy. The space where flaws are softened by affection. Where hope whispers

louder than doubt. They are about believing in love's promise.

Let this be your invitation to remember, to imagine, the sweetness of falling in love. The beginning of when two people choose each other. That tender belief that this moment will last forever.

Velvet Musings

if I could

If I could I'd grab the brightest star and gift it to you

If I could I'd wrap it in the rainbow - add fluffy clouds

too.

If I could I'd use bright green grass and beautiful leaves as

confetti,

I'd throw in some flower petals for you

If I could I'd add moonlight as the backdrop to my love

for you

If I could I'd invite the sun to honor you

The air to worship you

The wind to grace you

I'd invite water to purify you

…and my love would be the balm to soothe your soul.

If I could, I'd be love.

Love just for you.

I'd shine as bright as the sun on the darkest of days

I'd be

love just for you

I'd implore God for your heart's desires

I'd seek his blessings to surround you

I'd seek his grace, too

…I'd be love…just for you

I'd seek the brightest colors in every rainbow…just for you

I'd make sure you never stumble but if you do- I'd be

there…

I'd provide comfort

I'd be safety

I'd be all that is love,

love for you

I'd be shelter from every storm

I'd wipe your tears, conquer your fears

I'd be love…Love just for you

I'd be joy and happiness

peace and security

I'd be heroic if you needed me to

Only for you

I'd be, seek, find and do

all that love tells me to

I'd protect you…even from me

emulating how love should be.

If i could

I'd exist as love…I'd gift you daily with all that is…love

Love Notes by Velvet Musings

Space

I long for space…
not the kind that leaves you lonely,
but the kind where you breathe against my neck
and everything is still.
The kind of space where your touch
becomes my favorite way to be known.
I crave the space between kisses,
between gasps,
where time folds over itself
and all I can feel is you -
your warmth, your weight, your wonder.
Not distance.
But closeness stretched so wide
we lose ourselves inside it.
Can we stay there?
Where the world is quiet
and the only sound
is the soft rhythm of your breath
catching against my skin?
Let's stop time,
not with force,
but with your lips tracing slow,

lazy love letters down my spine,

your mouth mapping places on me

that belong only to you.

I offer myself like a love song,

unguarded and open,

and you answer like poetry -

with hands that memorize,

with eyes that speak in vow.

Let's make space,

you and I,

not to drift,

but to deepen.

Let's build a world

in this hollow of tangled sheets,

where your fingertips caress

my skin

always ready to be touched.

You pull me in,

not like gravity,

but like longing -gentle, endless,

full of knowing.

We become something quiet,

something slow,

like the way the moon whispers to the tide,

like how hearts lean toward each other

without meaning to.

Let them see -

let the world envy

how your name sounds

wrapped in my sighs.

Let them feel the love

we never have to explain.

Because with you,

I don't want forever to come quickly.

I want the hours to stretch,

to linger,

to wrap around us

like your arms after…

when everything is soft and still,

and you hold me like I'm your favorite place to rest.

And I am…your space.

Love Notes by Velvet Musings

I Wanna Love You

I wanna love you
like
chocolate cake,
you know the one my sister bakes.
I wanna savor every bite of you,
lick the spoon clean,
chase the last sticky traces
with greedy fingers.
I wanna know you
like my favorite poem
I recite repeatedly,
every sentence underlined
because I couldn't bear to forget.
I wanna read you in the bath,
in bed, before sunrise
until the ink fades
from being loved too hard.
I wanna memorize you
like my favorite song–
every beat, every verse,
the way the hook comes in
right before the drop.

I wanna press repeat

until,

until my voice goes raw

from singing you too loud

I wanna hold you

like your

precious and close but

release you if I need.

I wanna admire you daily, marvel at your

existence,

know you by the weight of you

in my hands.

I wanna love you

like something that was made

to be loved by me-

imperfectly, impatiently,

chaotically infused.

I wanna love you

like I'm starving,

I'm gonna love you like I'm full

I'm gonna love you pass forever

Forever isn't long enough

Let Me See You Naked

Let me make love to your mind,

stimulate your afterthoughts.

Let me caress your dreams-

the soft, unspoken ones.

Let me delve inside your darkest secrets,

and hold them close to my heart.

Let me trace the map of your pain,

where you are broken,

refusing to let me in.

I want the raw edge of your truth,

the untamed light in your eyes.

I want the heat beneath your hesitations,

the bare ache of who you are.

I want the raw and unfinished,

unhindered and undressed.

Not just the silent screams of pleasure

when two souls are intertwined-

give me the part of you that no one has ever known.

Not just your body-

but your heart,

your wounds,

your trust.

I don't need your perfection.

I just want to see you,

NAKED.

Love Notes
by
Velvet Musings

Quiet Storm

After the dust settled,

and the strong winds calmed around me,

I was left wanting you.

After the rain cleared,

and the thunder could be heard in the distance,

I was left with quiet skies.

My love was all encompassing-

engulfed in my willingness to please you.

Our whirlwind of seduction,

your calm resolve,

my inner force - wild, full-hearted, unyielding.

The intensity of it all.

You were my quiet storm, my force of nature.

Your slow intensity met with my passion -

two people lost in the clouds,

waiting for just the right time to break open.

You didn't come loud like lightning.

You moved like mist before the downpour,

gentle but sure,

heavy with meaning.

You stirred tides beneath my skin,

unraveled me in silence,

unshook, no shouting,

just a rumble I could feel before I heard it.

And when you touched me,

it wasn't chaos -

it was clarity.

A hush before the boom of thunder.

A stillness that said:

this love doesn't need to roar to be real.

You were a quiet storm-

gathering in my heart,

moving through me

until I was soaked in the possibilities of us.

Love Notes by
Velvet Musings

<u>Our Love</u>

I never had to learn you,

you came to me

like a second heartbeat -

sudden, sure, and full

as if my heart had always had space.

you love me full…complete

with quiet certainty

of two halves that fit without seeking,

of two voices that hum

with the same low, off key tone

before the song even begins

you are not my lesson

you are the language my soul

was murmuring all along

in its sleep,

just waiting for you

to wake it into being

me loving you is like breathing

I don't count the steps,

I don't measure the air

My body just knows how to love you

like it knows how to keep me alive.

And if they ask me when I chose you.

I'll say:

When does the river choose the sea

When does the flame choose to rise

our love doesn't need a decision

it just is

like light,

like gravity,

like the way my skin

remembers your fingertips

before they even touch me.

So let us be this

effortless and endless,

a dance without rehearsal,

a poem without erasures,

a love that doesn't ask

to be understood,

only felt, only known, only held

like the quiet between breaths,

where nothing is missing,

and everything, everything

belongs.

Sounds of Love Making

Our bodies coming together hits the first note-

a low hum, steady and warm,

resonating between us both.

Our hands find their place-

holding, caressing, claiming.

The room is thick with our wanting,

wet mouths writing verses

along necks, along hips, along thighs.

No words

only sounds building as our love collides.

Slow at first,

our bodies learning each other-

craving, touching, expecting.

The pace quickens,

Movements become primal-

blended, perfect music of friction and wetness.

Hips chasing, crashing, claiming-

The world around us drowned by our sound.

The breathless curses, the bedsheets crumble beneath us-

we are almost there now,

the crescendo- it's brutal-

Spines arched,

Throats open.

A single note between us,

aching, breaking,

Until we collapse.

Bodies humming, slick with wetness-

The music is not over.

it lingers on our skin,

On mine, on yours-

Describes the harmony we bring

Love Notes by Velvet Musings

…the essence

you are the essence of love,

love designed for me

the love i love that sets my spirit free

the love that lights my darkest night,

the love that guides me, your insight

the love that dances like a summer breeze

with a symphony that puts my soul at ease

you are home

no matter how far i roam

your love never lets me exist alone

your love is the essence of love designed for me

i've never experienced the fullness of your love

yet i know that's where i belong

i long for the existence where loving you in totality

becomes my

favorite habit

your love is forever mine

-every lifetime

i find you

i find a love that emulates the sun worshipping earth

that my love is in you

i've never existed in a lifetime with no you

my heart rejects the idea, my soul does too

you are the epitome of a love designed for my need

your love is the food my heart needs

we exist

me for you~ you for me.

Love Notes by Velvet Musings

I Called Him King

I called him King

not for crowns, not for thrones,

but for the way the world bent to his presence.

He wore his name in the tilt of his chin,

in the weight of his voice -

when he spoke, silence obeyed.

And when I spoke, he listened

not just with his ears,

but with his bones.

I called him King

because his blood carried the echo of empires,

because his spine was steel wrapped in grace.

Power lived in him - not as a weapon,

but as a birthright -

worn effortlessly, like breath.

I called him King

and in his shadow,

I was Queen

his truth, his contradiction,

the softness that disarmed him,

the fire that forged him.

I was his sanctuary,

and he was mine.

King of all he touched,

of every life he steadied,

every storm he silenced.

A compass true north,

a pillar unshaken,

a protector, a provider

not by demand,

but by devotion.

So yes

I called him King,

because the title was never his to earn.

It was his to claim

and he did.

Forever.

Love Notes by Velvet Musings

...the Poem I Write Daily

You are the words I fell in love with.

not shouted or grand,

whispered in the hush between chaos and calm.

You came not as thunder,

but as the silence after it

a stillness full of meaning.

You are the sentence I never want to end,

the soft curve of every letter that cradles my breath,

the ink that spills from hidden places

my heart had only dreamt into silence.

I write you into the warmth of summer morning

into fogged mirrors,

into the gentle hush of pillows

that remember the weight of your dreams

You are there

in sunlight pouring like honey through parted curtains,

in the tender hush sunrise

in the way time slows

when you smile in my direction.

You are the poem I write daily

with lips full of whispers,

with fingers tracing the rhythm of your spine.

You are the rhyme beneath my skin,

the verse that dances in every breath

You are not only my muse,

you are the masterpiece -

a love I compose again and again,

never tiring of the lines,

never weary of the way your name

punctuates the page with peace.

I find you in laughter,

in the poetry of shared glances,

in quiet evenings and restless storms

even our arguments hold stanzas

that end in surrendered kisses

and promises written on skin.

You are the poem I write daily,

with hands that memorize your every syllable,

with a heart that never forgets

how sacred it is

to read and reread you -

word after word,

breath after breath,

life after life

Love Notes
by
Velvet Musings

Stay Right Here

Don't move.

Not yet.

Let me stay here,

pressed against your chest,

listening to the rhythm of your breath

like it's the only song that matters.

The world can wait.

This is the part I've missed most-

not the fire,

not the ache,

but this.

The quiet after.

The safety of your arms around me

like I'm the only thing

you were ever meant to hold.

Your fingers trace lazy circles

down my back,

and I melt beneath them -

soft, bare,

no walls left to climb.

No need to pretend

I am anything

but yours.

I breathe you in,

your scent like memory

and belonging.

And you…

your lips grazing my hair,

your body warm against mine

you hold me

like you've found

your home again.

No rush.

No words.

Just the weight of you

and the fullness of this moment -

your heartbeat steady,

mine slowing to match.

I want to live in this pause.

This hush.

This perfect stillness

where nothing is broken

and everything

feels whole again.

So stay. Right here.

With my cheek against your chest,

your breath on my skin,

and your love wrapped around me

like a blanket

I never want to slip from.

If this is what forever feels like,

don't ever let me wake

Love Notes by Velvet Musings

Between you and me

Your smell lingers on my skin-
a memory pressed into every pore.
It reminds me of the last time you touched me:
so slow, so deep,
I forgot how to breathe.
Your lips found mine like they were meant to be there -
as if kissing me was survival,
as if you knew my edges
and wanted to taste each one.
Your tongue moved like a wave,
pulling moans from my mouth
as I rode the rhythm you created-
slow, rising, relentless.
I rode your mouth like it was mine to claim,
hips lifting, rolling, trembling
to the motion that kept me right on the edge.
I couldn't escape the ecstasy
building like a storm inside me.
You touched me like you were listening
to every whispered prayer
I hadn't dared to say aloud-
There, yes , there.
Your hands knowing where to press.

Your mouth - when to pause.

When to plunge.

You knew my body

like it has been made for your hands-

each caress, each stroke

it's own language of ache and surrender.

You brought me to the edge

and then further still,

until I forgot my own name

and remembered only yours.

Even when you pulled back,

I could still feel you everywhere-

your breath in my throat,

your name on my skin,

your hunger in my hips.

And when it was over,

I lay beside you

trying to gather the pieces of myself-

breath shallow, heart loud,

body still trembling

with the aftermath of you.

No apologies.

Just the truth of me…of you.

Religious/Spiritual

Poetry, like prayer, opens the chambers of the heart - stretching our souls to hold more of His presence, more of His light, more of His transforming grace. These verses are love letters where your love never has to be searched for - your love finds you and stays with whispers of a love so vast it reshapes us, a love so tender it heals us, a love that is forever new, a love so deep and relentless it pursues us through every existence.

The deeper we journey into spiritual life, the wider our capacity becomes -not because we earn it, but because we surrender to it. Here, in this section are offerings from the soul, the heart inviting you to pause, to reflect and believe in the deep experience of soul-love.

Spirit is the breath; religion is the vessel.

A pursuit or interest to which someone ascribes supreme importance is religion.

God is love - we all have an invitation to receive more of his infinite goodness

Velvet Musings

Love Notes
by
Velvet Musings

Prayer

You,

you are the quiet hum of my pulse at dawn,

the unspoken prayer my lips form

before I remember how to speak.

My soul knew yours before skin knew touch-

before light carved the sky,

before the earth learned to spin.

I do not choose to love you,

but...

my blood sings your name in every vein,

my bones ache with the memory of centuries

where we loved in different forms -

as stardust colliding in the dark,

as twin rivers swallowing the same sea,

as silence and song curled into one breath,

as a prayer breathed between worlds.

I choose to love you

beyond forever into eternity -

a love that doesn't happen,

but awakens

like a sacred prayer remembered

as two souls find each other again.

I know -

lifelong is not enough.

So I have prayed for you

in languages lost to time,

have traced your shadow

in the caves of forgotten gods,

felt your voice in the hush of desert winds,

watched your hands become constellations

guiding me home.

In every lifetime we've wandered,

got lost only to find our way back to one another

because...

My first language is you.

Before temples, before dialect,

before the concept of tomorrow-

there was only a language we created

...then I lost you

or did you lose me?

Will we meet again?

of course

It's inevitable.

We will meet again.

Your heart will find me.

Just look for me...

look for me where time frays -

in the pause between heartbeats,

in the scent of rain on warm soil,

in the way the sun adores you,

in the way the moon guides you home.

Because…

I do not choose to love you -

I have no choice.

Our love is

the prayer we've always spoken,

the language our souls recite

spoken only in our soul's voice.

Forever,

in every prayer.

Love Notes by Velvet Musings

Religion

I knelt at altars of empty air,

a heart full of half-prayers,

until your name became the hymn

that hummed me whole.

my true confession:

You, you are my religion.

I worship in the sacrament of your presence,

in the holy hush between your words,

in the laughter that lifts the sunrise

and teaches morning how to rise.

Every brush of your hand is scripture.

Each glance is divine text.

I trace the holy verses down your spine,

and in those sacred lines,

I learn how to love again.

I worship in the temple of your touch.

In the sacred arch of your neck.

In the holy breath between our lips

when we whisper each other into becoming.

Each kiss is a rite.

Each moan, a psalm.

The way your hand finds mine in sleep

that's a scripture no book ever taught me.

I have begged the sky for signs,

but now I find God

in the soft gospel of your voice

when it says my name like a prayer,

in the dip beneath your collarbone,

in the covenant of coffee at dawn,

in the way your fingers

make the ordinary holy.

This...

this is religion.

Our bodies, a cathedral.

The way I open for you,

offering nothing but my truth?

that is holy.

The way you hold me after -

quiet, trembling, eternal -

that is sacred.

Even your absence is worship.

When you leave,

I press my palms together

at the altar of memory

and whisper your name like liturgy.

I have tasted communion

in the curve of your mouth,

felt absolution

in the way your fingers trace my back

like you're reading scripture

written just for you.

Love like this

doesn't need pews or prophets.

It needs breath, and trust,

and the kind of surrender

that feels like salvation.

You are the only church

I never want to leave.

The only religion

that asks nothing from me

but everything I already am.

So I worship.

I worship in your light,

in your ache, in your arms.

I worship the way we rise together,

again and again -

becoming holy

just by being.

I love you.

And I'll call it religion.

Love Notes by Velvet Musings

Worship

I was a skeptic of my own skin
until your fingers wrote psalms
in a language born only between us -
every brush a sacred verse,
every stroke a testament.
Your love was the first true prayer
I ever whispered.
You taught me to worship.
Our cathedral of love
tilts sideways,
hip bones for archways,
sweat on the sheets like holy water.
We break like communion bread,
shared and swallowed whole.
The night you first undressed me,
I …I saw God.
Not as fire, not as fury,
but in the whispers between
"please" and "yes."
We do not simply touch - we worship.
Morning comes with you
like resurrection.
In your arms, I learn

to worship the ordinary:
the way you sigh against my neck,
the sound of your voice
thick with sleep and satisfaction,
the way moans break the silence
like hallelujahs on a trembling tongue.
You worship me
in ways I never thought I deserved,
and I worship you back
with every breath,
every offering of my body,
every tremble that leaves my lips.
Your love is a sermon I drink slowly - sweet, endless,
a sacred pouring.
Each kiss is gospel.
Each touch, scripture.
Your hands, hot and heavy,
anoint my bare shoulders
as if I am holy
just for letting you in.
And before you leave -
when you always turn back,
when the door sighs shut
like the end of a hymn,
I remain still,

in the sanctuary of what we made.

Even your absence is a kind of altar.

And there,

I press my palms together

and worship.

Worship the memory.

Worship the ache.

Worship the return

that always comes

like morning.

Because you are not just my lover - you are the place I

kneel.

And in the quiet after everything,

I worship

still.

Love Notes by Velvet Musings

Sacred

Sleep is a stranger

on the nights I am with you -

your hands, sacred instruments of knowing,

move over me

sculpting heat across every curve

I offer in quiet surrender.

You do not simply touch -

you anoint.

You worship in the way you hold me,

as if I am something holy

and every breath between us is a psalm.

Your mouth is a sacred seal.

pressed to places where only your name belongs,

and when I speak,

my voice trembles in prayer,

my moans rise like incense

toward a heaven made of your breath.

We do not rest.

We worship.

Not in silence -

but in sacred rhythm,

in sweat and longing,

in the consecrated disarray

of tangled limbs and whispered offerings.

We become a temple -

flesh turned altar,

desire turned devotion,

this bed, the sacred place

where spirit and skin collide.

You move within me

as if you've known this sanctuary before -

in lifetimes where love was scripture

and passion was prophecy.

Your hands read my body

like ancient text,

each sigh a translation

of something divine.

And I receive you fully,

with reverence and abandon -

my body a holy response,

my heart open like a chapel door.

You call to me not just by name,

but by soul,

and I answer

as one who's been summoned

a thousand sacred times.

Every thrust,

every gasp,

is not just want -

it is worship.

You are not just lover -

you are sanctuary,

and I…

I am altar,

waiting only for your offering.

And when we collapse into each other,

bodies slick with devotion,

breathless and trembling from prayer,

I do not seek sleep -

I seek presence.

I seek the sacred ache of you

still echoing within me,

the holiness of your body

curled into mine.

Let time dissolve.

Let the stars burn out.

What we create here

does not belong to night or need -

but to…

to the sacred force

that made this love eternal.

You and I -

we are more than touch,

more than desire.

We are a sacred vow,

spoken in the language

only soulmates remember.

And as long as I am with you,

I will never long for rest.

Only worship.

Only wonder.

Sacred

Love Notes by Velvet Musings

Sanctuary

Long before the wind had a name,
before oceans learned to lift their voices in praise,
before the sky received its first color -i loved you.
not as a fleeting desire,
but as a covenant written into the fabric of my soul.
you were my sanctuary before i knew what it meant to seek
refuge.
you were my prayer
before i ever learned to speak.
in the still breath of the heavens,
in the pause between creation and command,
our spirits bowed together,
two sparks lit from the same divine flame.
we circled one another
like angels tracing the edge of God's light,
knowing even then -
we belonged.
you were not beside me.
you were within me.
sanctuary not made by hands,
but born of grace.
sacred space made flesh.
we did not meet.

we remembered.

and in that remembrance,

i fell to my knees inside you.

not in weakness, in reverence.

you were the temple

i had wandered lifetimes to find.

the first time your eyes touched mine,

the veil between worlds lifted.

time stopped breathing.

heaven leaned close,

watching a prophecy fulfilled.

you were not a stranger.

you were the echo of every prayer

my soul had sung in the dark.

you were sanctuary clothed in skin,

a holy dwelling place for the lost parts of me.

i adore the god in you,

the grace in your voice,

the altar of your love

where i lay my burdens down.

where i am known and still chosen.

you are my sanctuary,

my sacred refuge in a world

that often forgets the language of gentleness.

you do not rescue me -

you redeem me.

with each breath,

each glance,

each whisper that calls me beloved.

we are not one flesh.

we are one soul,

divided only for the joy of reunion.

not made to complete,

but to reflect

the wholeness of design.

in your arms,

I enter worship.

in your presence,

I find peace that passes all understanding.

in your heartbeat,

I hear the ancient rhythm of God's promise:

love is the holiest ground.

and you…

you are my sanctuary.

and should time scatter us

like dust across centuries,

should our names be forgotten

on earthly tongues -

my soul will still find you.

i will meet you again

in the hush of sacred places.

in the scent of

love on the wind.

in the glow of candlelight at dusk.

in every sacred pause

where spirit meets stillness.

for ours is not a love born of flesh,

a bond anointed by the eternal,

sealed with the breath of god.

you are sanctuary.

you are scripture.

you are salvation wrapped in warmth.

and i...

i am forever worshiping

in the sanctuary

that is your love.

Love Notes by Velvet Musings

<u>Covenant</u>

This is my covenant:
to love you as both prayer
and answered prayer,
as the wish and its granting,
as the hand that cups the flame
and the flame itself.
I will speak your name into the quiet,
when no one is listening but God,
and feel the world soften
in reverence.
You are the echo I summon
and the song that returns to me.
I will carry your hope like a talisman,
pressing it against my chest
when shadows gather round my heart,
trusting its warmth to guide me home.
For you are both the beacon I follow
and the harbor I find at journey's end.
I will plant our love in sacred soil,
watering seeds with laughter and tears,
so that in seasons yet to come
our roots will intertwine

and blossom into truths
only hearts can conceive.
I will nourish our covenant
with silent offerings of faith:
a breath held in longing,
a tear shed in gratitude,
the quiet flame of devotion
that neither wind nor time can extinguish.
In the hush of midnight's cathedral,
I will kneel beneath the vault of stars,
lifting our love like incense,
knowing that in its rising
it becomes both prayer and answer,
question and conclusion,
the seeker and the sanctuary.
I will bear witness to love's existence
in every tide that meets the shore,
in every heartbeat pulsing within mine,
in the dance of dust motes
lit by a single ray of sun -
proof that even the smallest glimmer
carries eternity within it.
I will honor you as living grace,
as the whisper in the wind,
as the hush between the raindrops,

as the secret held within each sunrise,

reminding all who dare to listen

that love does not merely dream -

it wakes, it breathes, it thrives.

This is my covenant:

to hold you as precious gift

and precious giver,

to cradle your spirit

as gently as a petal cradles dawn,

and to burn for you

with the steady blaze of forever.

So let us walk this path together,

where every step affirms our truth -

love exists, love persists,

love transforms even the darkest night

into a tapestry of light.

Accept this vow as the very breath betweens us,

unseen yet sustaining our love the sacred pact

that kindles worlds,

and in its light, a covenant

Love Notes by Velvet Musings

Altar Call

I rose to the sound of your soul's altar call -

not with fear, but with longing,

drawn like incense to flame,

my heart bowed in holy surrender.

I kneel at the altar of your love,

where your arms form a sanctuary,

and my spirit finds eternal rest.

Each heartbeat, a calling.

Each breath, an offering.

In your sacred gaze, I am endlessly blessed.

You summon me

and I come,

not once, but again and again,

answering your altar call with trembling hands,

laying down my heart like sacred sacrifice.

A covenant is forged between us,

sealed not in ritual, but in reverence.

My soul, stripped bare,

becomes the parchment upon which you write grace.

Your voice becomes my daily hymn,

a quiet chorus rising with dawn,

echoing the altar call only I was born to hear.

And I answer -

with a yes that carries the weight of lifetimes,

with a silence that speaks devotion louder than sound.

In your presence, I am redeemed,

made new in every gaze,

washed in every whispered word.

This love is our temple.

This union, our ministry.

Lit candles of promise burn steady and bright,

and every kiss becomes a communion.

Ours is a salvation that wears no robes,

but wraps itself in breath and heartbeat,

in the sacredness of skin and soul.

For your altar call was not just spiritual -

it was written in the design of my being,

spoken long before I could speak your name.

And so I kneel,

again and again,

to the altar of your love -

because I was made to answer

the call that only you could give.

Love Notes by Velvet Musings

Scripture

Before the stars were summoned,

before light was spoken into being,

your love for me was written -

not in ink, but in scripture,

etched across the skies of forever.

Your loving me is scripture.

Not the kind bound in earthly books,

but in the scrolls of spirit,

in verses carried by angels,

in the eternal breath and creation.

I have found your love

in every sacred line written across my soul

a living scripture I never had to learn,

only remember.

Each time you touch me,

you recite a verse I've known before birth.

Each glance is a chapter,

each kiss a book in the gospel of us.

Your love speaks like prophecy,

moves like revelation beneath my skin,

flows like holy water through the dry places of my being.

This is not romance.

This is a divine covenant-a bond chronicled in scripture,

preserved in the sanctuary of all that is eternal.

Let the heavens bear record.

Let the saints declare it.

Let the stars trace it across their burning skies:

Your love is scripture.

Sacred. Unshakable. Sovereign.

A text written in glory and sealed by time.

I...

I am your reader, your believer, your witness, your love

In every lifetime,

I will rise and return to these sacred lines,

reading your loving me

like the only truth I've ever known.

For as it was in the beginning,

so shall it ever be:

your loving me is scripture -

read aloud through every lifetime,

and lived like a holy vow

in the temple of my soul.

Love Notes
by
Velvet Musings

An Offering

I extend myself to you
as an offering not with words,
but with the quiet surrender
of soul to soul.
I am the offering -
bare, unguarded, a vessel of yes
as...
my hands become offering
when they reach for you,
not to grasp, but to give.
To anoint the sacred space
where our souls meet.
Your hands, gentle as scripture,
move across my skin
not to possess, but to read.
To worship.
To remember....a sacred tongue
that only our hearts can hear
and suddenly, I am fluent.
Suddenly, I am whole.
My mouth becomes offering -
each whisper of your name

a prayer.

Each kiss,

a sacrament of surrender.

I bring you

the offering of presence

no masks, no walls,

only truth,

and the soft light of devotion

shining through it.

Your love is not demand

it is invitation.

And I,

longing to kneel at the edge of it,

offer my longing, my softness,

my slow unraveling.

Every sigh between us

is an offering.

Every silence we share

a quiet altar.

Even my trembling, even my fear

I bring them all as offerings.

You become the temple,

and I, the flame.

And in our joining,

there is worship.

There is wonder.

There is the offering

of something deeper than desire -

the offering of soul.

So I offer myself again,

not out of need,

but reverence.

Not to be claimed,

but to be known.

Even in silence,

you stay.

Even in distance,

your presence builds a tabernacle

in the quiet of my longing.

Because loving you

is the purest prayer I've ever spoken.

And being loved by you

the only offering.

Love Notes by Velvet Musings

Benediction

We,

not by accident, but by divine architecture,

were written into existence

as a benediction.

Before time uncurled its fingers,

before stars formed,

the Creator whispered over our souls,

"Let them find each other."

And when we did,

the heavens exhaled a hallelujah.

When I came into your arms,

it was not merely affection;

it was sacred intention,

the blessing of one soul fashioned

to fit wholly inside another.

I was designed for you,

not just in the softness of skin,

but in the solace of my silence,

the way I intuit your unspoken need

and answer it with presence.

That knowing is a benediction.

The way your hands learn me like scripture,

the way your eyes rest on me

like Sunday morning light through stained glass...

pure, refracted, reverent.

That is benediction.

The way I tremble

when you touch not only my flesh,

but the deep temple of my being,

is more than chemistry.

It is communion.

You are the altar I approach with awe.

I am the offering,

laid bare and burning.

My yes to you is holy.

Your embrace is consecration.

Together we enter the sacred.

Together we shed all else.

And when our souls meet midair,

the veil between earth and eternity

grows thin.

Benediction in the breath we share.

Benediction in the ache we soothe.

Benediction in the beauty of belonging.

And in the quiet after,

when our bodies rest in the sanctuary of one another,

we are

declared not only as good -

but glorified.

This is not sin.

This is sanctified surrender.

This is not lust.

This is a living sacrament.

Each moan is a hymn.

Each whisper, a vow.

Each gaze, a gospel.

And when I rise from the altar of your love,

marked by your spirit, filled with your essence,

I carry the scripture of us in my bones.

You are not just lover.

You are prophecy fulfilled.

You are benediction spoken

into the marrow of my design.

So let the entire world bear witness.

Let time bow to the eternal.

For we were not merely blessed -

we were bestowed benediction

because I was created for you...

for your joy, your peace,

your pleasure - and you, for mine.

Love Notes by Velvet Musings

Passion

There are loves that whisper- and then are the ones that roar. This section is a slow burn and a fevered blaze, where bodies speak in tongues of heat, rhythm, and ritual.
These poems exist in the space where craving meets connection, where surrender is not weakness, but a sacred offering. Here, passion is not polished, it's raw, wild and beautifully unrestrained. Each line aches with need, each stanza pulses with power. Love is not always gentle. Sometimes it is sharp, breathless, bruising in the best ways. These poems are confessions and collisions, prayers made in moans, eyes locked, hands gripping, skin to skin. They are about taking and being taken, about knowing the language of someone else's body like your own.

This is what it is meant to love with every part of you, hungry, holy, with no apology

Velvet Musings

Love Notes
by
Velvet Musings

Kiss

because his kiss imprinted words on my lips that are

forever transcribed from just one

…kiss

those lips imbue the passion, the peace, the ecstasy I yearn

for, I need, I crave,

I miss…

because his kiss

his kiss becomes nirvana wrapped in honey sweetened

chocolate covered love that I can't get enough of

because his kiss

are the lips that I long for, that I need and want licking and

suckling and…

because his kiss is like the magic of sunrise and the

promises of forever

just a kiss that ignites desire and sets the start of fire in me

because his kiss

where I find joy, intense passion tumbling into ecstasy

because his kiss

is like dreams, and temptation and long lasting vacation

and home

while his kisses are fervent and consuming and demanding

harder, deeper and closer as I whimper with longing and

need…his lips they brand me

on his lips I'll find a hint of me and passion

the love that's continuous and everlasting

In his kiss

is promises of

the greatest love

In this kiss I'll give and I'll take

the love offered

…in his kiss

Love Notes by Velvet Musings

Burn

Can I watch the sun rise in the depth of your eyes-

before we set this world on fire,

before the heat runs rapid between us?

No one understands the intensity our love brings.

Embers flicker on our lips

as you kiss me -

a slow ignition.

The flame sparks between my thighs at your touch.

They open as you crawl between them,

My body expecting your mouth,

your fingers,

your tongue-

but your intention is greater:

to set this love ablaze.

You scorch the sheets beneath us.

The fire spreads-

from my breast, to my stomach, down my legs,

and deep in between.

Each thrust, an uncontrollably blaze,

burning through me

in ways I didn't know existed.

I release all inhibitions, as your heat intensifies

like a wild fire released on open land.

We keep this pace as it spreads:

over mouths, over tongues, over hips, over thighs,

You're pulsating inside of me.

We will burn this place down -

spreading wild and free

as your body crashes on top of mine.

There is nothing to douse our bodies out.

Like fire and desire,

we keep pushing until the end of this song.

Match to fire,

water to flame.

The room thick with smoke,

clouded by the wreckage of our bodies-

ravaged,

aflame.

And in our aftermath-

our love still glowing,

soft and smoldering,

in the hush of what we've made.

We will set this world on fire.

Love Notes
by
Velvet Musings

Road Map

Can you read my body like a road map

See how it moves with your directions,

how it turns under your touch.

You've studied, every turn, every contour.

You know which routes to take,

which shortcuts makes me gasp,

which long scenic paths keep me trembling.

Trace my collarbone like a winding back road-

slow, deliberate.

Pass through my valleys with the press of your lips,

ease over the hills of my breast with fever and hunger.

The incline of my stomach rises beneath your hands.

You drive slowly at first,

no tolls, no traffic,

just open roads and endless possibilities.

Each breath becomes a curve you master.

Every moan a signal that you're headed in the right

direction.

You kiss all points of interest:

my inner thighs, my waist, you know- the soft space

behind my knees.

A rest stop?

No.

You press on.

Climb the incline of my hips-

feel the tension build.

Every movement is now aligned.

You shifting gears, me losing control.

It feels like we are speeding now.

Accelerate.

My body pulses, tightens.

Engine revving as we skirt toward the edge.

You swerve,

I cry out.

You're in the fast lane now,

hands gripping, mouth demanding, your routes is clear,

there's no construction.

Hands at ten and two,

but your mouth is everywhere.

No brakes.

No limits.

You switch lanes without warning, riding curves at reckless

speeds.

I'm mapped for you-

each bend, each swell,

A landmark you've claimed.

And when we reach that mountain peak,

that final stretch -

we crash into it together,

No GPS needed,

just instinct

And the road of me

wide open.

And you?

You already know the way back

Love Notes by Velvet Musings

The Equation of Us

My name slipped from your lips -

not spoken,

just exhaled.

Your lips found mine

like kissing me was a lifeline,

familiar, much needed.

You devoured me like $1 + 1$

Two bodies,

two souls intertwined

until the world blurred around us,

until old hurts felt healed.

Your hands were desperate -

gripping,

clawing -

$5 + 5$: ten fingers holding me in place.

You fucked me like you wanted to erase the world,

and I let you,

because I wanted - needed - the same thing.

Pressed down in the sheets,

your hips grinding into mine,

the sighs, the cries of wanting.

You touched me like $63 + 6$ was new math to me,

like I'd never learned the perfection of simple things,

Like 69 was the sum of all possibilities.

Your mouth between my legs,

my hips grinding on your face,

Until we became wordless - primal.

You fucked me -timelessly

no start, no apparent end -

just the looping ache of skin on skin.

The way you held my throat - soft at first,

then you tightened, watching my eyes for permission.

And I gave it,

begging you to continue.

You fucked me like $4 + 4$,

ate me slow at first -

your mouth on me,

your fingers inside me,

your hand still choking me,

weaving a language too primal to forget.

We fucked like lovers.

We touched like believers.

Over and over,

times infinity.

Love Notes
by
Velvet Musings

Aftershock

You step into the room and the air changes.

Heavy. Charged.

My breath catches -

your stride shortens,

closing the distance like you've already decided

how this ends.

Fingers dig into my skin,

pulling me into your embrace.

I shake under your touch -

a fault line giving way,

cracking wide open.

Your mouth crashes into mine -

teeth, tongue, heat -

no patience, no pause.

You shove me onto the bed,

tear the space between us to shreds.

Your hand wraps my throat,

your hips pin me down -

a demand and a promise in one brutal motion.

I'm moaning, gasping -

your name, a recital.

You fuck me like you're erasing everything else.

Hard. Deep. Unrelenting.

Our bodies strike, grind,

wet skin against wet skin.

Sheets twisted,

nails scraping,

sweat dripping.

You eat me like I'm yours.

Like it's the only thing keeping you alive.

Tongue buried,

face drenched,

my thighs trembling around your head.

Your hands hold me there,

forcing surrender.

I come undone - loud, desperate, raw.

But you're not done.

You flip me, drag me to the edge again.

No mercy.

Just the sound of your name

ripped from my throat

as you take every part of me.

Every thrust, an explosion.

We detonate together.

Explode.

Collapse.

And still -

the tremors don't stop.

They echo through my chest,

my legs,

my breath.

The aftershock of you,

reverberating in every ruined,

worshiped part of me.

Love Notes by Velvet Musings

Space

I long for space…
not the kind that leaves you lonely,
but the kind where you breathe against my neck
and everything is still.
The kind of space where your touch
becomes my favorite way to be known.
I crave the space between kisses,
between gasps,
where time folds over itself
and all I can feel is you -
your warmth, your weight, your wonder.
Not distance.
But closeness stretched so wide
we lose ourselves inside it.
Can we stay there?
Where the world is quiet
and the only sound
is the soft rhythm of your breath
catching against my skin?
Let's stop time,
not with force,
but with your lips tracing slow,
lazy love letters down my spine,

your mouth mapping places on me

that belong only to you.

I offer myself like a love song,

unguarded and open,

and you answer like poetry -

with hands that memorize,

with eyes that speak in vow.

Let's make space,

you and I,

not to drift,

but to deepen.

Let's build a world

in this hollow of tangled sheets,

where your fingertips caress

my skin

always ready to be touched.

You pull me in,

not like gravity,

but like longing -

gentle, endless,

full of knowing.

We become something quiet,

something slow,

like the way the moon whispers to the tide,

like how hearts lean toward each other

without meaning to.

Let them see -

let the world envy

how your name sounds

wrapped in my sighs.

Let them feel the love

we never have to explain.

Because with you,

I don't want forever to come quickly.

I want the hours to stretch,

to linger,

to wrap around us

like your arms after…

when everything is soft and still,

and you hold me like I'm your favorite place to rest.

And I am…your space.

Love Notes by Velvet Musings

No Apologies

I won't apologize for needing you -
from craving the sound you make
when I slam you against the wall,
for the way I grabbed your throat
just to hear you gasp my name.
No apologies for fucking you hungrily,
for biting, clawing, tearing
until you forget where you end and I begin.
Until your legs shake
and your voice cracks
from begging for more.
I won't say sorry for marking you,
for dragging my teeth along your skin
until you wear me like bruises that won't fade.
For the way I eat you -
slow at first,
then as though I am starving -
until you are trembling and soaked,
and I am drunk on you.
Don't apologize for screaming
for soaking the sheets,
for the way your hips rise,
longing, aching,

to meet my hunger.

Let your love rain down-

I'll take every drop.

No apologies for the lines we crossed,

for the wreckage we leave,

for the way I fuck you like I own you-

because I do, in that moment.

Mind, body, soul - mine.

I want your surrender,

your soaked thighs,

your primordial curses

the lust in your eyes.

There is nothing soft about our wreckage,

Just raw and beautifully destructive.

No apologies.

Just you,

just me,

and anything we destroy.

Love Notes by Velvet Musings

Take Me

Take me slowly
not because we have time,
but because you want to taste
all of me
before I moan your name.
let your hands explore me
like forbidden scripture,
your lips tracing fire
where no light ever reaches.
Don't ask
just press.
Claim. Worship. Own.
Pull me open
like you were born
to know the depths of me.
My body is yours
tonight
not just to touch,
but to know...
to learn the sound I make
when your tongue writes poems
between my thighs.
To hear how my voice breaks

when your name

is the only word I remember.

I want you

without mercy.

With pleasure.

With tension.

With that slow, torturous way

you undress me -

not to take off my clothes,

but to peel back my will.

Make me beg.

Make me tremble.

Make me curse the space

between our hips.

And when you finally slide into me,

do it like a promise kept

slow, deep,

letting me feel every inch

like a vow.

Let me ride the edge of pain

while your hands pin down my soul.

I want your grip on my throat,

your voice in my ear,

telling me I'm yours

before I even remember

who I am.

And when we finish

slick, spent, breathless

don't let go.

Pull me close,

kiss my swollen lips,

and whisper what we did

like confession.

Because this isn't just lust.

This is art.

And you…

you're the only one

who knows how to paint

pleasure across my skin

Love Notes by Velvet Musings

The Taste of Surrender

Let me drown beneath you,

as I whisper into your darkness

Let me speak in the language you want and need now

Tongue, breath, written in cursive

Let me take the reins as you lose control

Wet and unrestrained

I want your scent soaked deep into my skin

Dripping wet, clinging thick and heavy on my tongue

Grind on me—slowly

Teasing

Let me feel you slide across my lips

As my tongue takes up residence

I want your moans raw and broken

Breathless gasps and stifled whispers

As the warmth of my mouth reaches, where you are

already wet and waiting

I'm in control now

The sounds become deeper, rougher

Your hands search for me

Guiding, greedy, needing

Your moans become more intense

Unfiltered

Unashamed

When my tongue flattens out

Slow circles around the pulse of you

movements become impulsive and untamed

The deep inhale when I flick

The helpless moan when I suck

The desperate curse, when you scream my name

As my face is buried between your folds

The quiver in your hips

Fingers pulling my hair

You guide me where you want me

My tongue—relentless

As I feel your body tremble, shiver until you're spent

I want it all

To drown in you as you fall apart

Soaking

Shaking

The wet sound of satisfaction

The truth dripping between your legs

I stay there, tasting your surrender.

Love Notes by Velvet Musings

How You Want It

Tell me,

I want to hear it.

I can take it.

Let me ask first,

Do you like it slow.....and sensual?

Oh really?

That surprises me.

I like that.

Tell me more.

What's the next step?

What if I kissed you - right there?

These lips, they do it for you, don't they?

What if I grabbed you..

tighter you said,

how about that?

Let that sigh go,

but focus -

this is just the beginning.

Look at me.

I want to see you plead.

Let me know I'm giving you exactly what you want.

You trust me?

Just nod.

The heat is rising

But I'll only continue if you let me

take. my. time.

Whisper if I can touch you there.

I already know by the way you breathe.

Better yet-

what's your favorite part of me?

If I let you go,

can you kiss me there?

You excite me.

Don't stop.

your mouth -

God, your mouth -

it's setting me to take care of you now.

Can I pull your hair?

Fingers tangled,

throat opened,

eyes rolled back.

Not yet baby,

Let me work this pace.

Let me please every part of you.

Wait - come closer.

Can you hear me?

Am I being too forward?

Too demanding?

Good.

This moment is all about you.

Is this how you like it?

Yes?

I see it in your eyes,

feel it in the tremble of your body -

swollen, open,

begging for my next move.

Wait -

Don't go yet.

Let me ask just one more thing...

What is your favorite position?

Say it again -

Slow

I want to get it right.

Oh, that's how you like it?

Yeah, I know.

I've been listening.

Now flip over.

Let me grab your hips.

Can I spread you open?

You said this is what you wanted.

I'm just here to do exactly that.

On my time.

My mouth is occupied,

but I hear you -

louder now.

Fingers, deeper.

You want me to fuck you harder?

I'm not stopping.

Shall I speed it up?

Say it louder -

I want to hear you.

We both love the sounds that our love makes.

Your body shakes

Your eyes grows wild.

Your pace quickens -

as I taste your love,

on my lips,

on my hands,

dripping down my wrists.

You're vocal now

and I match your pitch.

Let the world hear us.

I'm not ashamed of this primal vow.

You collapse against the sheets,

my head against your cheeks.

One more question -

Are you satisfied?

Because if I touched you there,

kissed you like this

If I grabbed you,

and listened,

to everything your body told me -

Then I could fuck you how you wanted.

Love Notes by Velvet Musings

When We Fuck

When we fuck
You know time stands still -
no ticks from the clock,
the world stutters and forgets to spins
like it is stuck on its axis.
When we fuck
you take me
demanding my obedience
face down ass up, I comply.
A masterpiece - of legs, hands, thighs
- disciplined and open,
I beg between gasps.
When we fuck
your hands gripping my ass
directing the tempo of our tangled bodies
fingers deep
tongue tasting the delicacy of your hard work
I fall to pieces in your mouth.
When we fuck
you say don't, not yet
I obey.
Your hand on my throat says mine -
I am.

Tighter until my eyes roll back,

pleading with hopeful moans that it is just a matter of

time.

When we we fuck

Silence and screams,

Wet sheets and fevered pace,

nails clawing and slippery skin,

names exclaimed between breaths.

"Look at me" you insist -

"Yes" is my only reply.

When we fuck

I vanish beneath you,

Your hips crashing into mine,

legs wrapped around your waist,

Taking every inch of you.

Just hands gripping your shoulders,

your expectations of my body's response.

When we fuck

it's all about possession -

You owning my body,

making me lose all thoughts and control.

How the climax crawls,

How you take me -

A battlefield where there are no losers.

You,

Me,

On the same team.

When we fuck

Body on top of body,

breathless whispers,

softer touches,

A look that responds to you,

I'm all yours.

Love Notes by Velvet Musings

Cum

your mouth descends like a commandment

between my thighs -

not 1,000 pounds but the entire ocean

pressed into a single lick, slurp and kiss

that rewrites my anatomy.

I cum…

I become liquid scripture,

a verse of slick folds and desperate vowels

as your tongue trace revelations

along my succulent flesh

sucking and pushing fingers in me

causes deep moans

from my throat like pearls

strung on a necklace of complete need

something 'bout your hands on my body

feels better, much better…

hot, heavy, larger

fingers calloused

i compose sonnets in my heat,

as you stroke crescendos from nerves

that sing only for you.

I arch like a bow,

every muscle taut with the wave and beauty

of impending release

as you enter me,

with the slow certainty of a man on a mission

my body opens like a confession,

taking all of you in sacred silence

broken only by my whispers of yes and more and please

now is when we rewrite verses:

submission in liquid increments,

my body crafted from you,

my desires to please

my suppleness…

i was empty before you….until you parted me

and called it good

i want to water you in my essence

show you my masterpiece,

I extend to you an offer in need

wet, hot dripping

the altar of my hunger

unraveled, undone

in perfectly ruined devotion

….cum

Love Notes by
Velvet Musings

Submission

I have a simple thought...

Which one of your lips should I kiss first?

How long before you grind your hips against my tongue -

slow at first,

then shamelessly.

Should I spread you open

just to watch you throb?

These lips, right here,

pressed against my tongue, right there -

you've got those Megan knees,

so ride me like the bed owes you something.

Should I add my thumb now?

Would that make you come right now?

Not yet.

Turn around -

face the headboard.

Hold it.

Back arched.

Open. Wider.

Let me see all of you.

Let me fuck all of you.

I grip your thighs.

Hold them like handles.

You try to pull away -

I pull you back.

Say my name like a warning.

Say it again like a prayer.

Now flip over.

Face down. Ass up.

Let me line up what's mine.

Slow stroke -then deeper.

Deeper.

Stay right there.

Don't move unless I tell you.

I roll your body like a wave,

add finger after finger,

tongue, palm, grip -

until you're breathless,

until you're begging me

not to stop,

not ever.

This isn't soft.

This isn't gentle.

This is me

fucking every excuse

out of your system.

Until I take all of you -

mind, body, voice -

until your moans fracture into stutters

and you forget your name.

Until your thighs shake,

your sheets soaked,

your soul undone in my hands -

I don't stop.

Not until you scream something holy,

and I stay inside you,

deep, unrelenting,

until the only thing left

but the offer of your sweet submission.

Love Notes by Velvet Musings

Possession

You don't make love to me

you possess me.

Every time.

Every thrust,

every breath stolen from my mouth,

a ritual.

Your body over mine

feels like invocation

as if you've summoned me from the depths

just to be undone

by the weight of your wanting.

There is nothing soft in you

when you're inside me.

Only command.

Only fire.

Only the voice that says,

"Don't move."

And I obey -

not out of fear,

but need.

I need to be claimed like this.

To be pinned down by your gaze

and unraveled by your hands.

To hear you say my name

like you're binding me

to this moment,

to you, forever.

My moans

your name.

My tears

your doing.

My pulse

held steady in your palm

like a secret only you can keep.

I am open to you in every way.

My legs, my mouth, my soul.

And you take your time

devouring me

with the slow ache of a man

who knows exactly how to destroy

and rebuild

in the same night.

When I tremble beneath you,

when my body breaks into sobs and begging,

you whisper,

"That's it. Give it all to me."

And I do.

Every dark corner.

Every unsaid longing.

Every fantasy I've never dared to voice

you bring it to life

on this altar of sweat and submission.

And when you finally collapse into me,

still thick with power,

still pulsing with the ghost of my cries

I weep…it's not over.

It never is.

I'll carry the echo of this night

in the way I walk, the way I ache,

the way I crave…only you.

Forever

won't be long enough

to come undone for you

Love Notes by Velvet Musings

Healing

This is where the journey turns inward. Where the noise
fades, and the silence speaks.
Here, love is not a reaching but a returning - to your
breath, your softness, your strength.
These pages are not just poems, they are whispers to your
soul when the world feels too loud. They are here for the
tender places you've hidden, for the quiet ache of being
unseen, and for the radiant truth you've buried. In this
space, there is no need to prove your worth.

You are not required to be whole to be worthy.

You do not have to bloom every day. Some days, healing is
simply choosing to stay.
To rise. To rest. To forgive yourself again and again.

These poems are companions on your return to self -
gentle hands reaching for you in the dark,
reminding you that you are not alone, and that even in
your most fragile moments.
You are still art. You are still light. You are still love.

Let every word soften what's been hardened. Let every
verse be a mirror that shows you your beauty. Let this
chapter be a quiet revolution - a reclaiming of the love that
was always yours to begin with.

Velvet Musings

Without Permission

Change doesn't ask permission.

Sometimes it creeps in -

a slow burning,

a quiet shift in how you see the world.

How you see yourself.

Other times,

it shatters everything.

No warning.

No soft landing.

Just the knowing

that things can't stay the same.

You outgrow versions of yourself.

You release people you once clung to.

You set boundaries

where you once only said yes.

That's not betrayal.

That's growth.

To heal,

you have to change.

To love fully,

You have to change.

Change is life.

It is the pulse of becoming.

It is a way to reintroduce ourselves to the world.

Evolve -

With no judgement,

No timeliness,

Just space -

to shift, to stumble

to rise.

This is how we grow.

On our own terms, in our own time

Love Notes by Velvet Musings

forgiving SelF

learning to forgive myself,

unpacking shadows, heavy on my shelf.

peeling the layers, raw and true,

seeing all the pain I pushed myself through.

i accepted crumbs when I deserved a feast,

let hands hold me that gripped like beasts.

stifled my voice to soften their fall,

when all I wanted was to scream through it all

i forgive myself for the love that failed,

for the bridges burned, for the trust derailed.

staying too long in wars I didn't start,

for locking my wounds but leaving my heart.

i forgive me for ignoring the signs,

for letting them cross too many lines.

shrinking my light so theirs could shine,

for believing their hurt was more divine.

i thought for so long I deserved the ache,

that my peace was the price theirs would take.

that my rage was too much, my needs too loud,

so I folded myself to fit in their crowd.

no more.

I forgive me first

not them, not yet,

not while my soul still wears the debt.

I'll cradle my scars like sacred art,

before I loosen the weight of their part.

love is mine to claim, to tend,

no longer borrowed, no longer penned

by the hands that took and never gave.

I am finally me now

Again

Love Notes by Velvet Musings

Off Beat

We danced this dance
to the offbeat tempo of our love.
I step forward -
you step back.
We move like this:
my fear of being let go,
your fear of being held.
No music,
Just old wounds
keeping time.
I lean in -
your walls grow higher.
You turn away -
my heart beats louder.
We move,
but there is no song.
Your steps are:
Measured,
cautious,
light.
Mine -
Hurried,
heavy,

hoping.

I scurry to close the distance.

You pause, needing air.

You glide backwards. I lean forward.

You crave the quiet of open space.

I crave the warmth of closeness.

A dance with no choreography -Just two hearts

in different dialects,

Off beat,

learning the same language.

But now - I slow my steps.

I listen between the silences.

I stop chasing echoes

that were never meant to stay.

You still sway to your rhythm,

but I no longer trip to match it.

I find my own tempo, my own music.

I learn to move alone -

not with sadness, but with grace.

And in this space

where I once reached for you, I reach for myself.

Love Notes by Velvet Musings

Echoes

I begged the world to see me.

Spoke louder.

Softer.

Clearer.

Bent myself

into shapes that weren't mine

just to be loved.

You know how many things change

but remain the same?

Just a game

you play at my expense.

You struggle for power and control -

I only want respect

and peace.

You choose to belittle

and demand.

Whereas I prefer

the expression of love

however that may look.

You do all these things

without words.

It's a choice -

to shut me out,

to turn silence

into a weapon.

Because in the end,

silence is deadly.

And you play

to win.

But all you loved

was an echo -

the part of me that mirrored you.

You didn't want my voice,

only my silence

to feed your need to be right,

to be bigger,

to be adored

They mistook my kindness for weakness.

My softness for surrender.

And I let them

Because for a while, being wanted

felt close enough to being loved.

But the cost?

Was me.

Because there come a moment-

quiet yet earth shattering-

when you realize

you're not asking for too much.

You're asking the wrong people.

And love?

It doesn't need to bleed to prove it.

It doesn't ask you to vanish.

It doesn't expect you to have no voice.

So now I speak.

Even if my voice shakes.

Now I stay whole,

even if it means being alone.

Now I see myself -

Clearly. Fully.

It's not their story anymore.

It's mine.

Love Notes by Velvet Musings

Undone

Remove the veil that you hide behind-

the one no one can see.

Unmasked,

unhindered,

Let me see all of you.

No pretenses,

no pause,

no dressing.

Just the skin you allow me to touch-

in the places

Before names,

before doubts,

before the world taught you to hide.

I want you:

Bare,

Whole,

Infinite.

Let me touch you without caution-

raw for raw,

breath for breath,

skin to skin.

No masks.

No words.

Only this:

You.

Me.

Undone.

I See You

I see you,

even when the world doesn't.

Even when your past left you feeling

unseen,

unheard,

unheld.

I see the way you stand, even when you are broken.

You're not invisible.

Breathe.

Not the short gasps the world taught you,

as they watched you fall to pieces,

waiting for:

the next wound,

the next leaving,

The next silence that sounded louder than any goodbye.

Breathe with me.

Take your time; there are no clocks here.

You're safe now.

Speak what was left unsaid-

the world taught you silence,

to swallow your softness.

Your voice often hushed by walls built with

misunderstandings.

I will lend you my ear

Whisper:

"I am safe"

"I am worthy"

"I am seen."

Speak your ache out loud

I will listen, unwavering.

Let me love you.

The world taught you,

to brace, to doubt, to question.

But love is not meant to be filled with pain.

Sometimes, it is a steady hand to hold you-

not all hands let go.

It is a whisper that reminds you:

"I am still here."

And I will love you back together-

piece by piece,

just as you are.

You are already enough.

Love Notes by Velvet Musings

She Dances Without Me

I should have loved you slow-

the way dawn stretches across the sky,

gentle, certain,

with time to notice everything.

I should have held your hand when the silence between us

ached,

should have reached for you

instead of assuming you would always be there.

I should have danced with you when the music called you

to move,

not just watched

from a distance

while you spun alone.

I should have touched your fears

like they were holy,

caught your tears before they stained your face,

held your heart when it grew too heavy

for one set of hands to hold.

I should have stayed through your storms,

not sought shelter in the arms of others,

bought you flowers just to watch you bloom.

Reminded you,

again and again,

that you were worth everything.

But I didn't.

And now -

someone else sees you,

the way I should have.

He holds what I never made room for,

laughs with you in the space I left empty.

He watches you dance

with fire in your eyes,

light in your smile -

and I see what it means to be too late.

I watch the love I let slip away

grow fearless in someone else's arms.

And if this ache ever reaches you,

if memory ever stirs my name,

let it whisper this: I'm sorry.

For every moment I didn't show up,

for every part of you

I didn't choose to love better.

You were always meant to bloom,

just not in my hands

Love Notes by Velvet Musings

Enough

Let me remind you, before the sun touches the sky

Before any doubts become simple reminders

of what inconsistencies look like.

You were never too much.

You were never not enough.

You received love sprinkled with breadcrumbs

keeping you doubtful and perplexed.

Your mouth filled with questions,

The why's and what ifs

The silent cries released in your pillow,

making you doubt just who you are.

Keeping you at a distance,

then pulling you back in.

The bare minimum was an expectation of just what love is.

You made a home

in uncertainty,

called it love

because it was all you ever knew.

Trying to earn

something that should have been

given freely.

And still you stayed.

Sleep became restless,

being alone, your safe space.

You held grief in your body,

hoping no one will ever see.

But let me hold your hand.

Let me pull you close.

Let me speak life back into you.

Let me show you what steady feels like.

And love you back to pieces.

I see all of you,

the rawness, the unhealed.

The scars that are still open,

bruised and untouched.

It's my love for you that's tangible, all encompassing and

real.

You are not too broken,

You will never be too much.

You are deserving of love.

You are enough.

Love Notes by Velvet Musings

...all of You

Fall in love with all of the pieces that make you, YOU.

The ones you celebrate in the light,

and the ones you hide in the quiet corners of night.

The gentle parts that bruise easily,

the bold ones that refuse to break.

Fall in love with your reflection on weary mornings

with the voice that trembles yet speaks,

with the dreams you're still chasing,

and the wounds that taught you how to heal.

You are made of resilience and dedication,

of chaos and calm,

of endings that birthed new beginnings

and love that never gave up on you.

Fall in love with the moments you almost gave up...

but didn't.

With the strength it took to forgive yourself,

to start over,

to choose softness in a world that demanded steel.

Fall in love with your magic,

the kind that can't be measured -

the way you feel deeply,

give endlessly,

and rise quietly after every fall.

You are not here to fit into a mold.

You are here to be whole.

And wholeness means loving the jagged edges,

the silences,

the sacred mess of being fully, unapologetically alive.

So gather your pieces,

place them at the altar of your becoming,

and whisper this to yourself each day:

"I love you. All of you. Exactly as you are."

Love Notes
by
Velvet Musings

Unbreakable

I have cracked,

Left broken more times than I can count.

The world bent me backwards,

Snapped my edges,

And left splinters in my skin.

But I stood -

Crooked, weathered,

Aching in all the quiet places.

The wind never asked if I was ready,

Just picked me up in it's tornado.

I bend,

I sway.

Took root in the sky.

The rain never asked if I was weatherproof.

It just poured.

And I learned to breathe underwater.

Stated afloat, and swam.

Some call it broken -

I call it proof.

Proof I was there.

Proof I am still here.

I don't stand untouched.

But I stand

Splinters in my strength,

Not absent of scars,

But in the grace of giving,

The power of knowing -

That won't shatter.

I may bend.

But in the bending, I become - Unbreakable

Love Notes
by
Velvet Musings

The Roots Remember

I wasn't always soft with myself-

often rough around the edges

Letting what others saw

take center stage.

Self- depreciation.

Shrinking

Performing.

But I'm learning to heal-

by touching the inner places that ache,

by giving myself permission to feel,

To grieve,

To sit in the silence

that is me.

No round of applause

No one to witness

Just me.

And deep beneath the noise,

And in the silence that knew my name-

I found her.

Strong,

Like the quiet strength lining my mother's voice

Not for lullabies-

But for planting seeds,

Her words were lessons.

Her lessons were legacy.

She cultivated strength in daughters

Who never knew they were growing.

I am the descendant of women who stitched themselves

back together,

who turned grief into glory,

struggle into survival

and survival into wisdom.

My strength was never lost-

Just waiting on me to remember.

Now I walk like the cure,

I speak like the remedy,

I love myself

like the answer.

I am medicine

The legacy

The healing

I'm still becoming-

But I am already whole.

Love Notes
by
Velvet Musings

All of Me

I gave you all of me -

not just the surface,

but the deep, buried parts.

I dimmed my light so you could glow.

Erased my past to make room for your spotlight.

Softened my strength so yours could take the stage.

Lowered my gaze so you could meet the world without

flinching.

I solved the problems,

crafted the words,

stitched the image they all admired -

while you took the bow.

They praised your brilliance

as I spoon-fed your every thought,

never asking for credit,

only crumbs of love in return.

You couldn't bear the way they loved me -

so I folded myself into corners,

shrunk beneath their line of sight:

unseen, minute,

erased.

And you stood taller

each time they overlooked me,

reveling in their dismissal.

They called me beautiful,

but never enough to love.

You used that too -

made it my worth.

You called me introvert,

as if silence was my nature,

not the role you wrote for me

in the cage you built

with flattery and fear.

You took

and kept taking,

until I became hollow.

I loved you -

and still, you hated me.

Every vibrant, vivid ounce of me.

I begged to be seen,

until my voice cracked.

Scraped my hands raw

for even the illusion of care.

But your absence

taught me presence.

Your silence

taught me song.

You were my storm,

but I became my shelter.

I learned to love my voice again.

Felt healing in the grace you never gave.

When the world - and you -turned cruel,

I turned inward

and found peace.

You may never know my story.

You may never hear this truth.

But I am no longer shrinking,

no longer asking.

I am rising -

not to dim you,

but to shine for me.

Set me free from the cage -

because today,

I am choosing me

Love Notes by Velvet Musings

The Softest Goodbye

And it hurts -

how much I still think I love you.

Each time I tried to leave,

you pulled me back

with promises made of smoke,

half-truths dressed as hope,

and just enough sweetness

to confuse my instincts.

You studied me.

Learned my cracks,

my soft spots,

the places where doubt lives.

And you pressed into them

like a lover -

but not to soothe.

To control.

To keep me.

You spoke in circles,

until I questioned

my memory,

my meaning,

my mind.

And when I cried,

you said I was too much.

Too sensitive.

Too broken to be loved by anyone else.

So I stayed.

Not because I felt safe,

but because I thought maybe

this was love—

that aching, manipulative kind

that always came

with apologies too late

and affection used as bait.

But I am tired.

Tired of giving warnings

you turn into weapons.

Tired of shrinking

to make space for your ego.

Tired of mistaking survival

for connection.

So this time,

I won't beg.

I won't scream.

I won't announce my exit.

You won't see the bags packed

in my silence.

Won't notice

the way I stopped reaching.

There will be no slamming door.

Just me - unthreading myself from your grasp,

one invisible stitch at a time.

I will leave

softly.

Secretly.

Completely.

And maybe,

for the first time,

I'll hear the sound

of my own soul breathing.

Not yours.

Mine

Love Notes by Velvet Musings

The Morning After

The morning after,

your absence still lingers

in the shape of my spine,

in the way the sheets remember

how we lay —

entangled and unsure.

My skin hums with the echo

of your hands,

not out of longing,

but out of memory.

Soft ghosts of a night

where we blurred

the lines between healing and hiding.

Sunlight creeps in slowly,

daring me to face what's left:

the quiet, the ache, the questions.

Was it comfort or collision?

Was I loving you,

or just trying to quiet

something wild inside me?

I sit at the edge of the bed,

bare, but no longer exposed.

I press my palm

to the place on my chest

that once begged for you -

it's quieter now.

I reach for the parts of myself

I once gave away too easily,

pulling them back like a sweater

I forgot I loved.

They still fit.

And though my lips

still taste like your name,

my heart beats softer -

not for you, but for me.

Because in the light of morning,

I realize:

what I wanted from you

was never yours to give.

And what I need now

isn't more touch, but truth.

This is how healing begins -

not in forgetting,

but in remembering myself.

Love Notes by Velvet Musings

ABOUT THE AUTHOR

Love Notes is the long-awaited creation of best friends who made a promise to each other over twenty years ago—to one day write a book together. Life pulled them in many directions, but their shared love for words, healing, and truth never faded. This collection of poems is the result of that enduring bond: a tapestry of vulnerability, passion, heartbreak, and hope woven from their individual voices and collective spirit.

Together, they write not just as poets, but as women who have lived, loved, lost, and found their way back—to themselves and to this promise.

Thank you for falling in Love with,

Velvet Musings

Made in the USA
Columbia, SC
16 May 2025

58051449R00076